C000279377

STAR WARS

COLLECTIBLES

A Pocket Guide
by Stephen J. Sansweet

RUNNING PRESS
PHILADELPHIA • LONDON

Library of Congress Cataloging-in-Publication Number
97-76130

ISBN 0-7624-0322-5

This book may be ordered by mail from the publisher. Please include $1.00 for postage and handling.
But try your bookstore first!

Running Press Book Publishers
125 South Twenty-second Street
Philadelphia, Pennsylvania 19103-4399

INTRODUCTION

I didn't set out to build the largest
private collection of *Star Wars* stuff . . .
but it didn't just happen, either. I was
so totally blown away by George Lucas'
epic space fantasy the first time I saw
it, that I just had to have some
reminder of its power and its fun close
by. But did I want the R2-D2 ring or
the C-3PO version? Instead of making a
hard choice, it just seemed simpler to
buy both. Soon both rings became all
rings, and all rings became everything.
Out of such small initial decisions,
entire collections are born.

One of the bad things I've learned about having a truly large collection of anything is that it isn't very portable. Also, when you add two floors onto your house for your collection, it becomes clear that it controls you, not the other way around.

This book is a small response to both of these vexations. It is truly portable and, by forcing me to select a few dozen of the coolest, weirdest, or most representative items from my collection of more than 25,000 *Star Wars* products, artifacts, and bits of memorabilia, it gives me some sense of control.

Just as *Star Wars* revolutionized the movie business, it also changed licensing and merchandising in major ways. There had never been a truly successful movie/merchandise tie-in until Lucas and his company changed the rules. Since it first premiered in 1977, *Star Wars* has been a truly global phenomenon—as it soon becomes clear while thumbing through this book. From ticket stubs and bottle caps in Japan to Australian ice cream on a stick; from an R2-D2 cookie jar to a Chewbacca tankard . . . these are a few of my favorite things. Enjoy!

—*Steve Sansweet*

In 1978 Kenner feared that sales would be low for the Jawa—the smallest figure in its original 12-character *Star Wars* line-up. (It was only about half the size of the largest figure, yet it cost the same $1.97.) So executives made the decision early in the run to replace the

cheap vinyl cape with a "richer-looking" cloth cape. Today, the cloth-cape Jawa sells for more than $100. But mint-on-card versions of the "cheap" vinyl-caped Jawa have sold for more than $2,500, making it the most valuable of the 115 figures offered between 1978 and 1985.

AUTOGRAPHS

Authentic George Lucas autographs are hard to come by, but my friend Eric Hansen knows this one is real. He showed up on the British set of *Return of the Jedi* in 1982 with a photo of George and Chewbacca from *Star Wars* and got it inscribed in person. The toughest *Star Wars*-related autographs, besides Lucas, are those of Harrison Ford (Han Solo) and Sir Alec Guinness (Obi-Wan Kenobi).

To Ezra
Keep the faith
Geor...

11

BADGES

This set of pinback badges from *Return of the Jedi* shows a heroic Ewok, Luke and Leia, Darth Vader, and a strange image of C-3PO and R2-D2 seemingly suspended in space before the business end of a Star Destroyer. They were for sale at Japanese movie theaters in 1983.

Whether it's Imperial or New Republic credits or just plain nickels, dimes, and quarters, these ceramic banks of C-3PO, Darth Vader, and R2-D2 produced by Roman Ceramics in 1978 make handsome receptacles.

BELT BUCKLES

Heavy as paperweights, these original brass belt buckles by Leathershop Incorporated were among the first licensed items from *Star Wars* back in 1977, an era when wide, custom-fit leather belts and choose-your-own clunky buckles were all the rage.

STAR WARS

C-3PO
R2-D2

STAR WARS

DARTH VADER

BOOKS

This Taiwanese edition of the *Return of the Jedi Sketchbook* has a more striking cover than the American version, but it is also notable for another reason. Even though George Lucas had changed the film's title a year before, this book still refers to the film as *Revenge of the Jedi*.

反攻 電影畫冊

精采彩色劇照近三十幅
超水準設計圖二百餘幅

Bottle caps from Coca-Cola, Fanta, and Sprite in Japan carried 50 tiny color photos of characters, vehicles, and scenes from *Star Wars*. The plastic tray to keep them in is quite rare—but rarer still are the caps that customers turned in for instant cash rebates.

BOXER SHORTS

What a difference a generation makes! During the original trilogy, the only *Star Wars* underwear was for kids, mainly Underoos. But today, manufacturer Ralph Marlin outfits adults with boxer shorts like these.

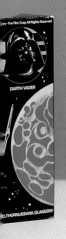

What could be more incongruous than a marshmallow in the shape of Darth Vader, as in these 1978 Mallo Shapes from England? How about Australian frozen treats on a stick? Ice cream surrounds a center of "Jedi Jelly!"

The crews working on the *Star Wars* trilogy got T-shirts, patches, and hats with each film's logos. Today, *Revenge of the Jedi* material is the most collectible, along with *Blue Harvest*, the cover name for *Jedi*. This proposed metal mug for the cast and crew never made it into production, making it one-of-a-kind. Just in case there was any doubt, it bears a helpful reminder: "Filmed on Earth."

Sigma created ceramic figurines for *Return of the Jedi* in 1983 and 1984, which are part of a larger collection of beautifully sculpted and colored music boxes, bookends, teapots, salt and pepper shakers, photo frames, candlesticks, string dispensers, and even a landspeeder soap dish.

They may have
tasted a bit like
sugared card-
board, but the
1984 boxes for
C-3POs cereal by
Kellogg's sure
looked cool, with
masks on the
back or special
trading cards
and plastic rock-
ets buried inside.

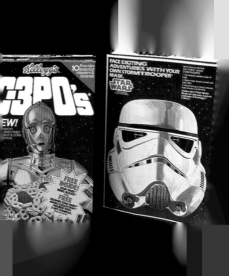

These six coin designs were produced in two weights of silver and
two weights of gold by Rarities
Mint in 1987 and 1988. But,
based on the smallest mintage
of three of the coins
(Vader/Kenobi, Han Solo/
Chewbacca, and R2-D2/
C-3PO) there can only be
14 complete sets of all
24 coins. The asking price
for an entire collection of these
Star Wars 10th Anniversary
medallions is $25,000! And that
doesn't include the equally rare
one-tenth ounce gold coins sold
only as part of necklaces in Japan.

A near-mint copy of the first 1977 issue of Marvel Comic's *Star Wars* series (there were 107 monthly issues in all) can be worth anywhere from $15 to more than $350 depending on the cover. This is the rarest version of #1, featuring a 35¢ test-price on the cover with a UPC code at the lower left. Marvel only printed a few thousand. The other copies from the first print run were marked 30¢. Reprints with a cover price of 35 ¢ don't have the UPC bars.

35

COOKIES

Chewie! That seems like a pretty good way to sell a cookie, but Luke Skywalker and Darth Vader? These 1983 Pepperidge Farm *Star Wars* cookies molded in the shapes of some of the most popular characters in the trilogy came, in vanilla, peanut butter, and chocolate flavors.

While George Lucas **didn**'t think much about merchandising **when** he was writing the script for *Star* Wars, the cracker barrel shape **of** R2-D2 led him to muse that it might make a fun cookie jar. In late 1977, this ceramic jar and its metallic companion from Roman Ceramics landed in pantries throughout America.

With so many aliens and masked characters, the trilogy was a Halloween natural and a huge seller for Ben Cooper from 1978 through 1985. By the end of the run, there were 16 different costumes available including this rare Klaatu vinyl kids' costume from 1983. Note that it's imprinted with the third film's abandoned title, *Revenge of the Jedi*.

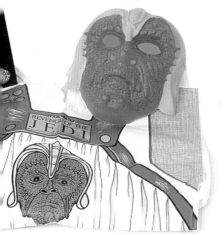

The Coca-Cola Company was a promotional partner for the trilogy around the world. It worked with theaters, convenience stores, and fast-food chains to supply such items as this 1978 set of eight colorful cups, free with the purchase of a soda or frozen slush drink. One cup front is shared by mortal enemies from the planet Tatooine, a Tusken Raider and a Jawa.

Kenner Products' die-cast metal vehicles became an instant collectible when they were released starting in 1978. The line included these three vehicles from the Imperial fleet: Darth Vader's TIE fighter, a TIE bomber, and a regular TIE fighter. For reasons that even Kenner can't explain, the TIE

bomber was produced in relatively low numbers, and one mint in the package today can command more than $600 while the others go for about a tenth of that.

Even at the kitchen table there was no escaping the pervasive influence of the hugely popular films. This 1983 plastic *Return of the Jedi* dinnerware from Deka includes a partitioned platter, soup bowl, cereal bowl, cup, and lidded decanter. Today these items are fairly easy to find at flea markets.

Among the most unusual product tie-ins was this 1983 campaign in Australia for Harper's Dog Chow. Then again, perhaps it isn't so strange when you consider that the Wookiee Chewbacca was modeled after George Lucas' dog Indiana. The Vader decal on the bag informs dog owners that there's one of 12 *Jedi* stickers inside amongst the beef-flavor kibble.

There's a mighty
RETURN OF THE JEDI
**CHARACTER
STICKER**
inside this pack.
Collect all 12 in the series.

Meaty Beef Flavour

100% Complete
& Balanced
Nutrition

**Dog
Chow**

Harper's
Pet Chows

49

Kenner called them "large action figures," but the public called these products averaging 12-inches "dolls." The tallest and last-issued regular figure was the bounty hunter droid IG-88. The line was discontinued after 1979 when the *Star Wars*-loving public showed an overwhelming preference for the 3¾-inch action figure line.

FLYING DISCS

These flying discs with
Star Wars decals are
from a 1978 mail-in offer
from Pine Sol disinfec-
tant. While a few
of the designs
aren't that difficult
to find today, a
full set of six in
mint condition
is an elusive goal
for the true enthusiast.

For the junior Jedi in training, what could be better than a *Return of the Jedi* desk and chair set from American Toy & Furniture? The 1983 line included a rocking chair, bookshelf, and toy-toter/clothes hamper in the shape of R2-D2.

Some board games translate well, such as Kenner's 1979 "Escape from the Death Star" game, available in Italian, German, English, and Japanese. Other Kenner/Parker Brothers board games include "Destroy Death Star," "Adventures of R2-D2," "Battle at Sarlacc's Pit," and "Ewoks Save the Trees!"

Initially, Kenner wasn't going to make any *Star Wars* weapons because of the anti-gun tenor of the late 1970s.

But George Lucas insisted, and the toy company produced a small Han Solo blaster and this all-purpose stormtrooper/snowtrooper electronic laser rifle. Made for all three films, this rare *Jedi* version was available only from the J.C. Penney Christmas catalog in 1983.

These 1997 half-scale helmets from Riddell, which makes full-size helmets for the National Football League, are even more carefully designed than the original props, most of which had no detailing inside. The Vader helmet and mask break into three parts to show the Dark Lord's breathing apparatus.

60

Among the first items to hit stores in 1977 in the wake of the unexpected huge success of *Star Wars* was a line of jewelry from Weingeroff Enterprises that included rings, earrings, charm

bracelets, necklaces, tie tacks, and these girls' barrettes, which feature R2-D2 and C-3PO, the film's version of 'Laurel and Hardy.

In a 1978 mail-away premium offer, you could redeem a Cheerios boxtop to get this plastic and wood *Star Wars* kite. Today's collectors would likely prefer the intact Cheerios box to the kite itself, because of its rarity.

LUNCH BOXES

Before plastic achieved its current lunch room supremacy, the trilogy spawned these lithographed metal

lunch boxes from King-Seeley Thermos. Each came with a drink thermos decorated with a *Star Wars* decal.

One of the first licensees, Don Post Studios, is still on board today, turning out such high quality replicas of character masks that some were requisitioned for use in the filming of the new *Star Wars*: Episode I. This deluxe Darth Vader mask from 1996 was molded from one used in the making of *The Empire Strikes Back*.

There were more than three dozen plastic model kits issued by MPC in the United States alone between 1978 and 1985. These C-3PO and R2-D2 model kits from the first year of production were assembled and painted by talented modelmakers at Industrial Light & Magic for use as presentation pieces.

The first *Star Wars* film crew patch had stylized lettering that was eventually replaced by the more familiar logo. The logo was teamed with the Norwegian unit stripe for the filming of the opening sequences of *The Empire Strikes Back*. The depiction of Darth Vader in flames in a later patch seems a strange choice for a film in which he was triumphant. The Yoda patch was used before the change of name for the third film, *Return of the Jedi*.

For many years, this small metal pencil sharpener first produced by Helix of England in 1978 was the only three-dimensional replica of the Death Star.

The Japanese have used—and collected—phone cards for many years. In 1987, Panasonic issued *Star Wars* 10th Anniversary cards as part of an advertising campaign for audio and visual equipment.

Trilogy plates from the Hamilton Collection in 1993 had artistic montages from each of the films, fitting in memorable characters, vehicles, and even scenes.

This 1979 Cantina playset was part of Kenner's regular line. An earlier cardboard version exclusive to Sears came with a Snaggletooth figure that was too tall and dressed in blue instead of red because the only reference the toy-makers had was a black and white photo showing the creature just from the waist up.

84

The cuddliest part of the trilogy—
Ewoks—became plush or "stuffed" toys.
Here are Kenner's Wicket W. Warrick
and his friend Princess Kneesaa from
1983.

POPSICLES

The beautiful graphics on a 1983 ten-pack of assorted flavor Popsicles from Pauls in Australia are an adaptation of the American theatrical poster art by Tom Jung.

Pop-up books fascinate young and old alike, and are a hot collectible in their own right. This 1996 *Mos Eisley Cantina Pop-Up Book* from Little, Brown has the complete bar-room along with a chip that produces that famous, funky music and the sounds and lights of laser fire.

89

For the foreign release of *Star Wars*, marketers decided to use different "key" art than the main image used in the United States. Foreign posters featured more action, with explosions, guns blasting, and a shimmering lightsaber. This dynamic 1978 Hong Kong poster uses new art by Tom Cantrell.

George Lucas' special effects work-shop, Industrial Light & Magic, made this lightweight resin laser pistol for Harrison Ford's use in *Return of the Jedi*. It was used when the gun was holstered, making it much lighter than the cast metal version used for close-ups. Authenticated props from the trilogy rarely come to market since Lucas decided to keep and archive most of them. One of the few that have been auctioned, an authentic Darth Vader mask, brought $20,000 for a Lucas-endorsed artists' rights foundation in 1993.

Obi-Wan might tell you "These aren't the droids you're looking for," but these could be the jigsaw puzzles you seek!

They were the first of more
than a dozen boxed puzzles Kenner
released in 1977 and 1978.

THE EMPIRE STRIKES BACK
10th Anniv. YODA 1980-1990
Sculpted by L. NOBLE
Produced by KILNCRAFT ENTERPRISES
for LUCASFILM LTD.
© 1990

This 8-inch tall bronze Yoda **by** artist Larry Noble was the first *Star Wars* limited-edition sculpture. This statuette was one of only 50 numbered pieces produced by Kilian Enterprises in the late 1980s.

Built for speed, these 1983 jet-black roller skates from Brookfield Athletic are one of the few products to carry illustrations of the red-garbed Imperial Royal Guards.

These blue nylon *Star Wars* slippers were available only from the British retailer Marks & Spencer in 1978.

SODA CANS

Soda cans from Wisconsin to Thailand
helped get the word out in 1997 about

the *Star Wars Trilogy Special Edition* as part of a worldwide promotional tie-in with PepsiCo.

SWITCH-PLATE COVERS

We'll never know how many thousands of lights got turned on and off by tweaking Darth Vader's mask, C-3PO's face, and R2-D2's body with these novel 1980 Kenner Switcheroo light-switch covers for kids' rooms.

These silver foil stamps and canceled regular postage stamps use key art from the 1995 video release of the *Star Wars* trilogy. They are legal postage for mail in the Caribbean island nation of St. Vincent and the Grenadines, but it's safe to say that few ever graced envelopes there.

Among the first *Star Wars* collectibles offered, these handsome ceramic tankards from California Originals in 1977 were sculpted by Jim Rumpf. The Chewbacca mug, in particular, is one of George Lucas' personal favorites.

This 1983 C-3PO cellophane tape dispenser from Sigma offers a novel way to tear off tape—and an assured laugh line when Threepio actor Anthony Daniels in mock indignation describes to convention audiences how it works.

Illustrated movie ticket stubs and advance discount coupons for the 1997 opening of the *Star Wars Trilogy Special Edition* films are prized collectibles in Japan.

スター・ウォーズ

前売ご鑑賞券 ¥1600

¥1600

新宿文化シネマ

シネマ　新宿文化シネマ
☎03(3)54124091

Among the most attractive packaging
for a trilogy product are these 1980
boxes of Puffs facial tissue that pro-
moted the opening of *The Empire
Strikes Back*
with photos
and art
depicting
scenes
from the
film.

119

This card doesn't exist . . . officially. It was supposed to be promo number P3 for the 1994 *Star Wars* Galaxy II trading-card set from Topps, but Lucasfilm ordered all copies destroyed because George Lucas had never said whether there was, in fact, a species of Yoda-like beings. The few copies that have escaped shredding have become collector's gems. Since 1977, Topps has done 24 trilogy trading card sets.

Emblazoned on the front of this 1977 *Star Wars* T-shirt from England is an iron-on decal of the Hildebrandt Brothers classic key art for the first film.

Among the strangest of action-figure-sized *Star Wars* vehicles is this 1979 Imperial troop transporter, which didn't appear in the movies. The transporter boasted several "original *Star Wars* sounds," but it was really designed for holding a bunch of action figures. Kenner made 20 large vehicles in this scale in all, including the alphabet soup group of A, B, X, and Y-wing fighters.